Jiminy

Alice

Daisy

Tramp

Simba

Peter Pan

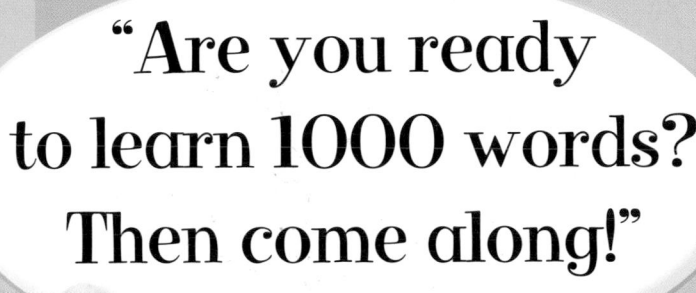

"Are you ready to learn 1000 words? Then come along!"

Jasmine

Lilo

Donald

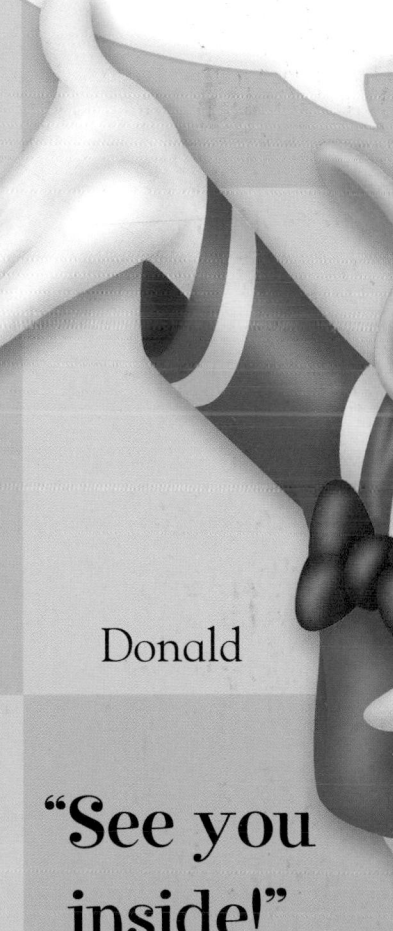

Aurora

Buzz Lightyear

"See you inside!"

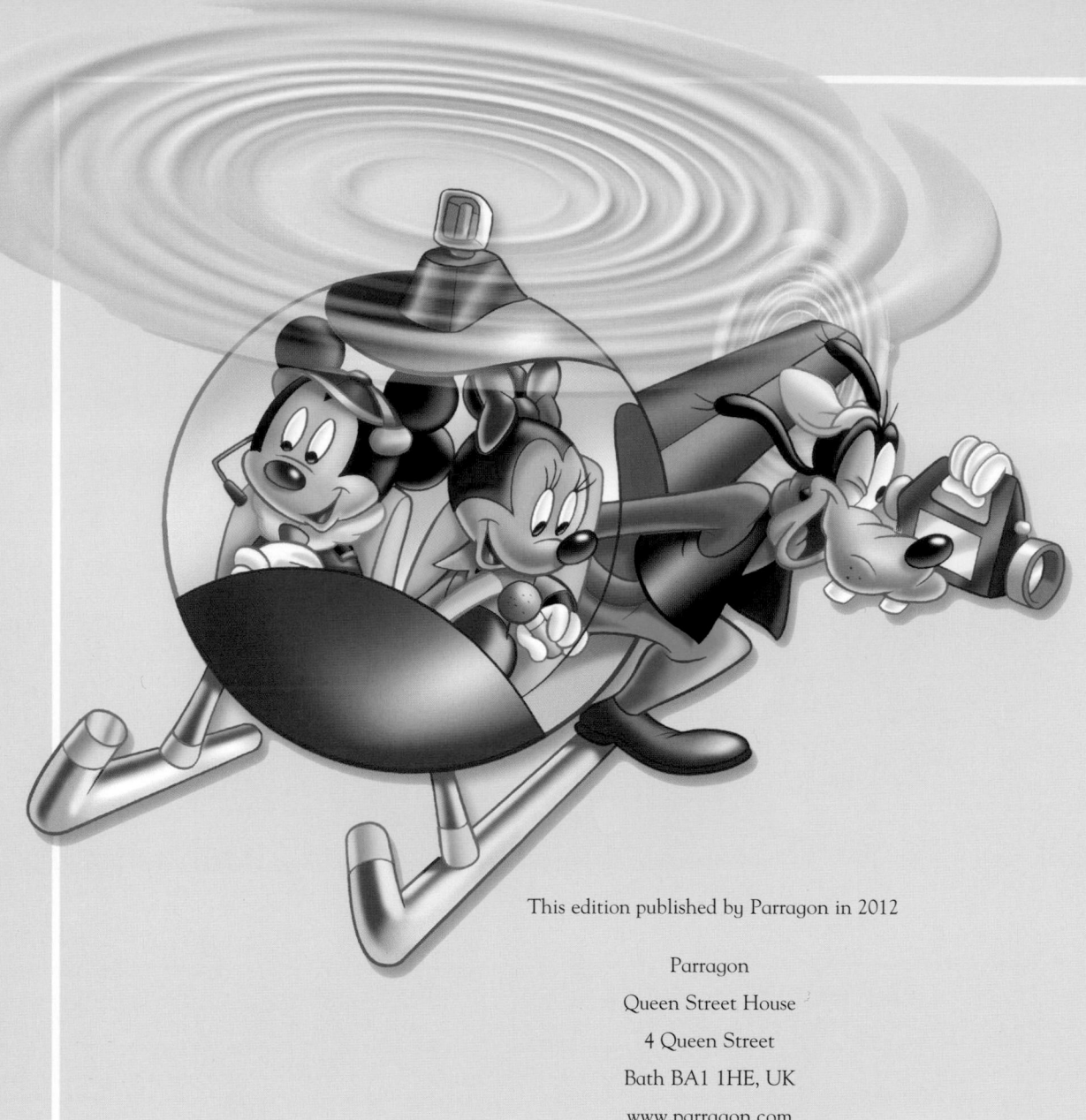

This edition published by Parragon in 2012

Parragon
Queen Street House
4 Queen Street
Bath BA1 1HE, UK
www.parragon.com

Written by Thea Feldman

ISBN 978-1-4454-6675-0

Printed in China

ʤisney

My First 1000 Words

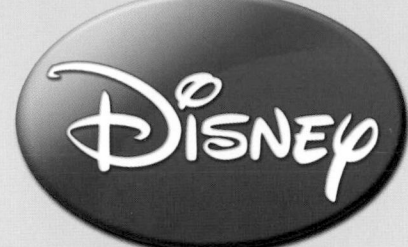

PaRragon

Bath · New York · Singapore · Hong Kong · Cologne · Delhi
Melbourne · Amsterdam · Johannesburg · Auckland · Shenzhen

Dear Parent,

This book is filled with more than 1000 first words to help young children develop their vocabulary, so they can describe and explain the exciting world around them. The words in this book have something for every inquisitive young mind, helping your children increase their confidence as they move through their everyday world and fuelling their imagination for places and things far away.

The book is divided into five major subject areas, with each chapter introducing another theme. Favourite Disney characters invite young children to join in with the action. **My First 1000 Words** is designed to be a family experience, enabling parents to help their children make valuable discoveries and also to find out that learning is fun and easy when carried out with the help of Disney characters.

Table of Contents

Home and

"There you are! We've been waiting for you."

Family

Turn the page to see what's going

on at Mickey's . Find out who meets

a new . Discover all the things growing

in 's garden. Help  tuck in.

And, needs your help in the kitchen.

But beware! Look who loses

his temper when you find him

in the .

All Kinds of Families!

How many family members do you have?

father
mother

brother

sister

brother

the Darling family

daughters

father

daughters

Ariel's family

queen   king

princess

Sleeping Beauty's family

husband

granddaughter

wife

pets

the Dalmatians' family

mother father

grandmother

Mulan's family

uncle

Donald's family

nephews

mother

child

Dumbo's family

Mickey's House

clothes

lawnmower

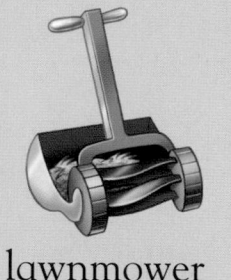
kennel

window

garden

chimney

roof

porch

fence

"I'm glad you came to visit me!"

house

nails

front door

saw

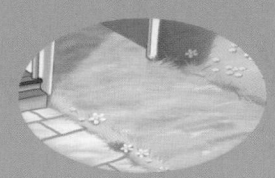
drive

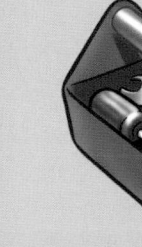
toolbox

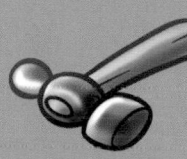
hammer

garage door

car

letter box

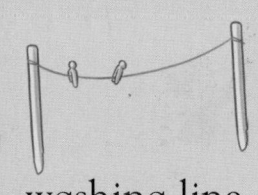
garage

washing line

wood

birdbox

Daisy's Garden

"It's fun to make things grow!"

14

wheelbarrow

seeds

plants

worm

vine

water

soil

rake

cane

watering can

sprinkler

seed packet

hedge

trowel

CAN YOU FIND?

five snails

hose

sunflower

15

The 101 Dalmatians' Living Room

fireplace

armchair

television

floor

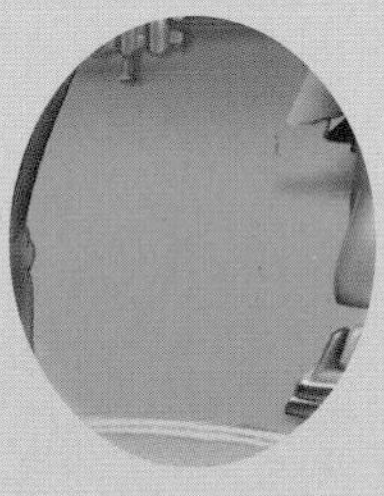

"It's time for our favourite programme!"

CAN YOU FIND?

three bones

wallpaper

footstool

clock

lamp

light switch

banister

rug

vacuum cleaner

settee

bookcase

books

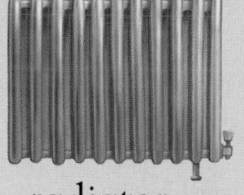

radiator

vase

coffee table

lampshade

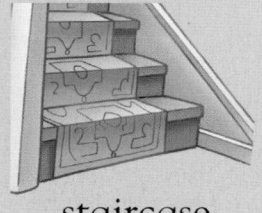

staircase

Lilo's and Nani's Kitchen

measuring jug

mop

saucepan

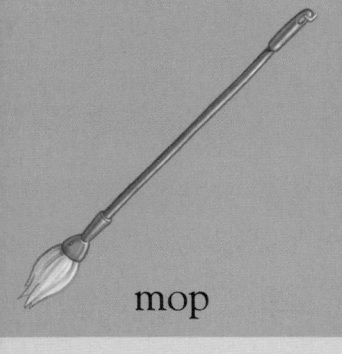
refrigerator

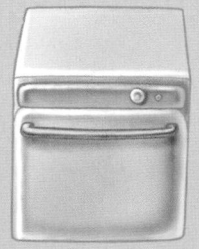
dishwasher

"Help me stop all these bubbles!"

frying pan

rolling pin

sponge

kettle

sink

 blender

 cupboard

 soap suds

 oven

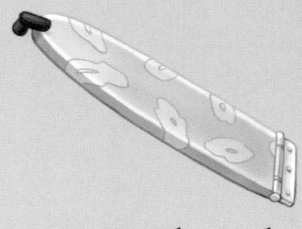 ironing board

 tea towel

 tap

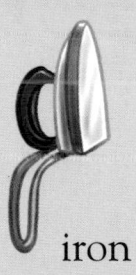 paper towel

 iron

rubbish bin

CAN YOU FIND?

three mugs

 toaster

 stove

 apron

dustpan

 brush

Beauty and the Beast's Dining Room

cup

dish

knife

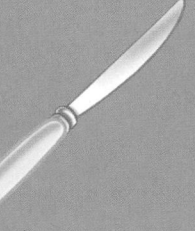

plate

table

"Be our guest! Dinner is served!"

spoon

jug

fork

saucer

china cupboard

napkin

chandelier

sugar bowl

teapot

glass

CAN YOU FIND?

a salt pot and a pepper pot

candlestick

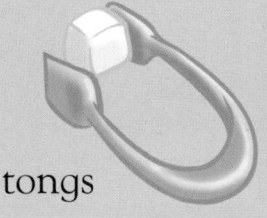

tongs

place mat

milk jug

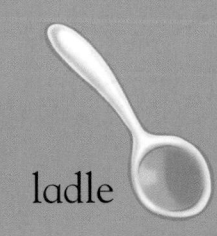

ladle

bowl

Dinner for Two for Lady and the Tramp!

spaghetti and meatballs

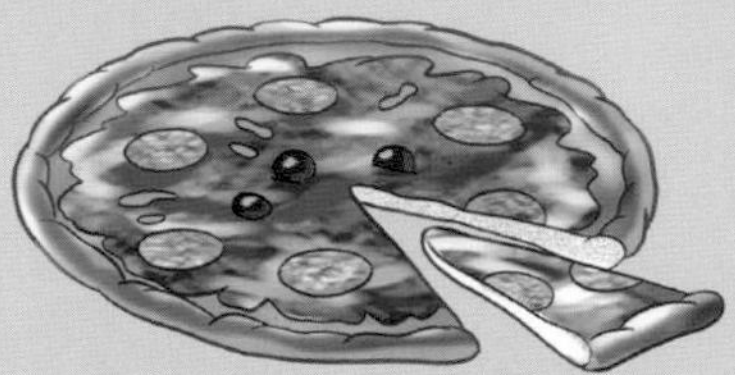

pizza

rice

pasta

soup

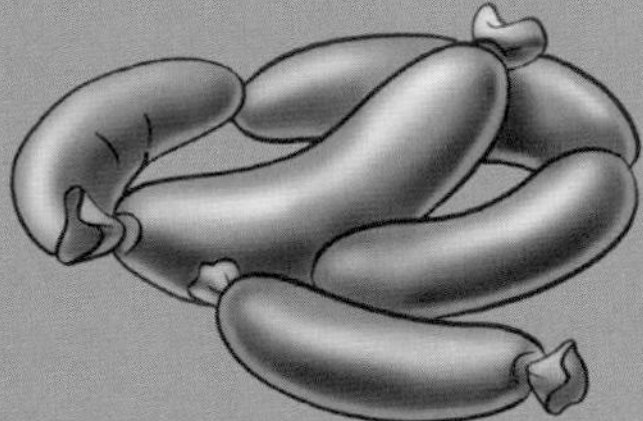

sausage

toast

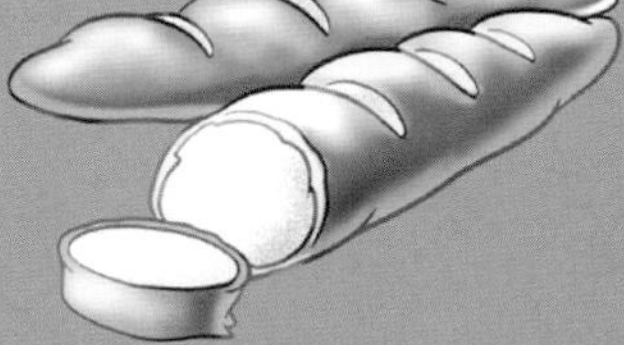

baguette

crackers

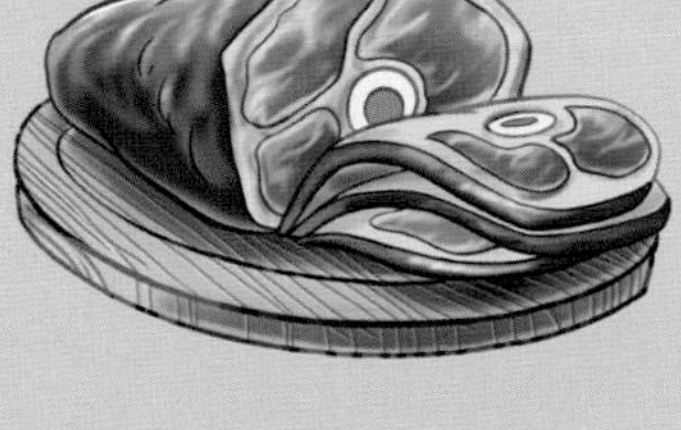

ham

jam

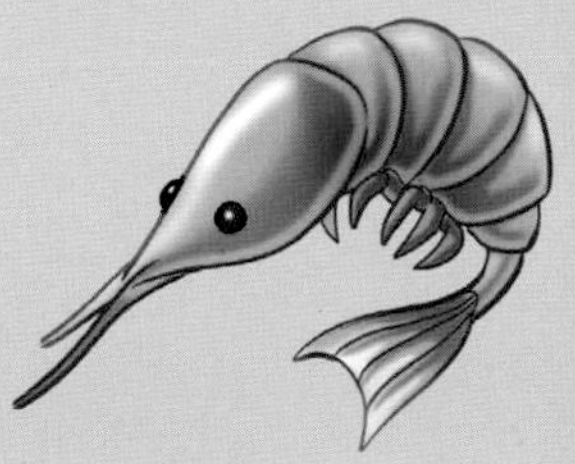

prawn

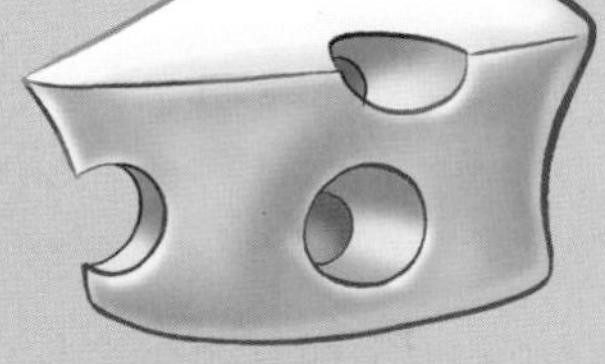

cheese

milk

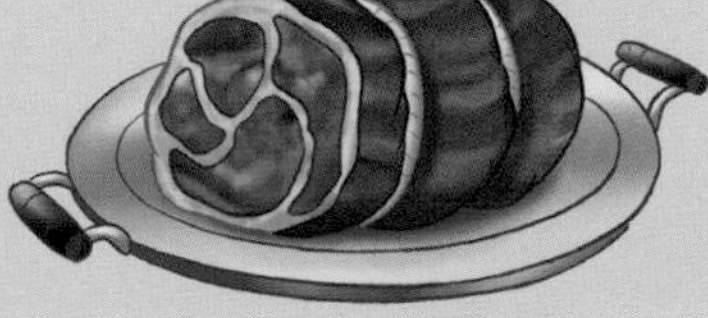

roast beef

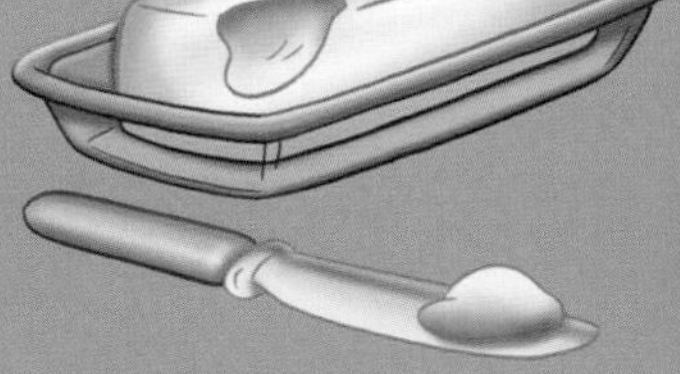

butter

22

eggs

tuna

sandwich

lobster

bacon

peanut butter

steak

yoghurt

hamburger

cereal

salt

pepper

chicken

sauce

"Which are *your* favourite foods?"

chips

tea

23

Snow White's Apple and a Feast of Fruits

apple

banana

cherries

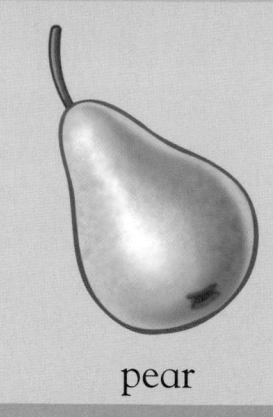
pear

melons

strawberries

raspberries

blueberries

blackberries

watermelons

mango

avocados

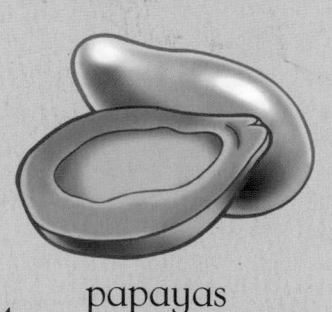
papayas

pineapple

peach

plums

raisins

coconuts

oranges

grapefruit

grapes

lemons

limes

"Take a bite, my dear."

A Pumpkin Takes Cinderella to the Ball!

garlic

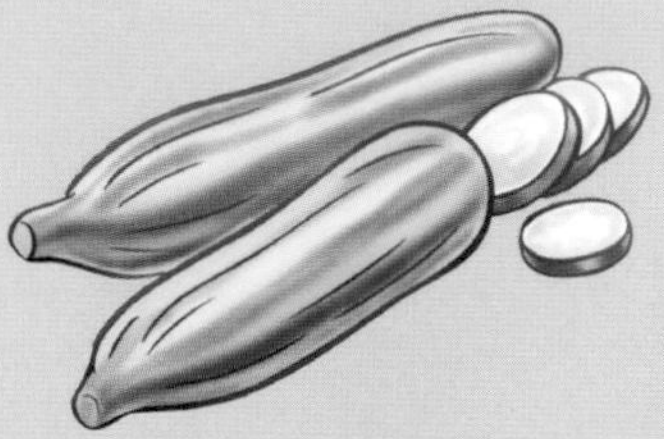

courgettes

aubergine

lettuce

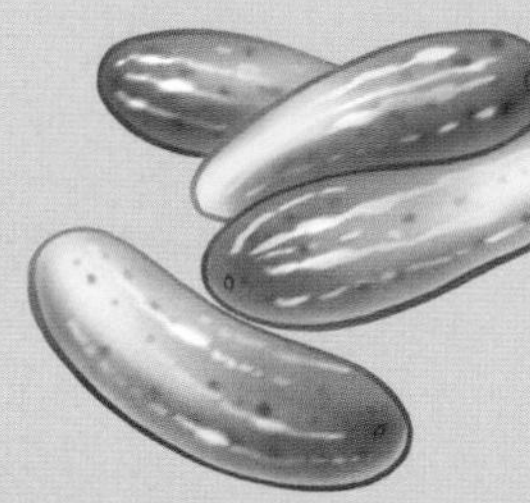

gherkins

beetroot

"Be home by midnight, before the coach turns into a pumpkin!"

olives

cauliflower

spinach

Brussels sprouts

radishes

celery

peppers

broccoli

tomato

cucumber

potatoes

French beans

beans

onion

pumpkin

cabbage

carrots

sweetcorn

peas

mushrooms

Donald's Bathroom

bathrobe

medicine cupboard

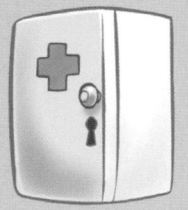

soap

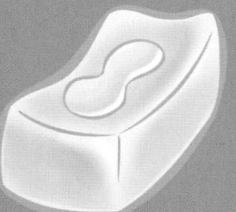

hairdryer

"You're in my bathroom!"

hairbrush

comb

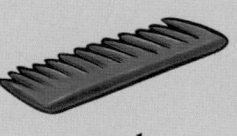

toilet paper

towel rail

bubbles

bath towel

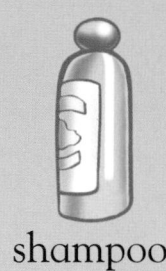
shampoo

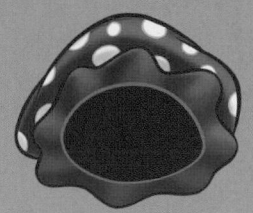
shower cap

flannel

shower

toilet

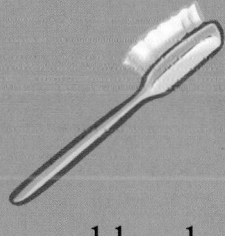
toothbrush

CAN YOU FIND?

three rubber ducks

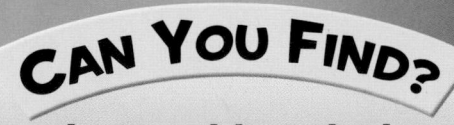

mirror

yacht

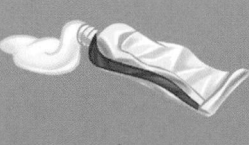
toothpaste

nailbrush

bath

29

Babysitting in the Nursery

pram

mobile

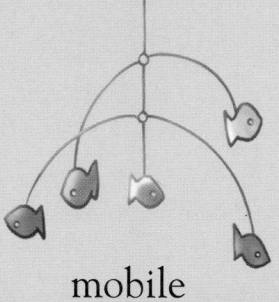

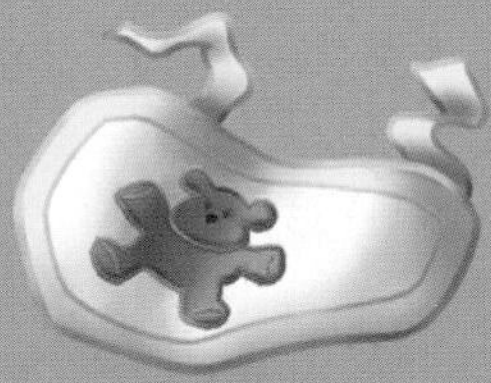

bib

rocking chair

"Look . . . it's a baby!"

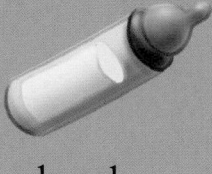

bottle

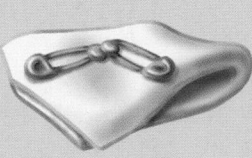

nappy

teething ring

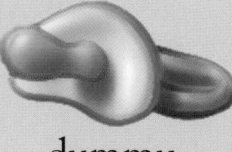

dummy

with Lady and the Tramp

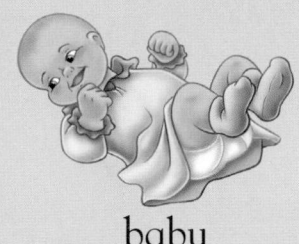
baby

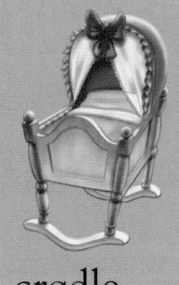
cradle

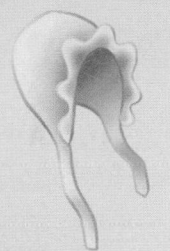
bonnet

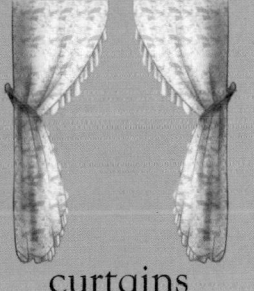
curtains

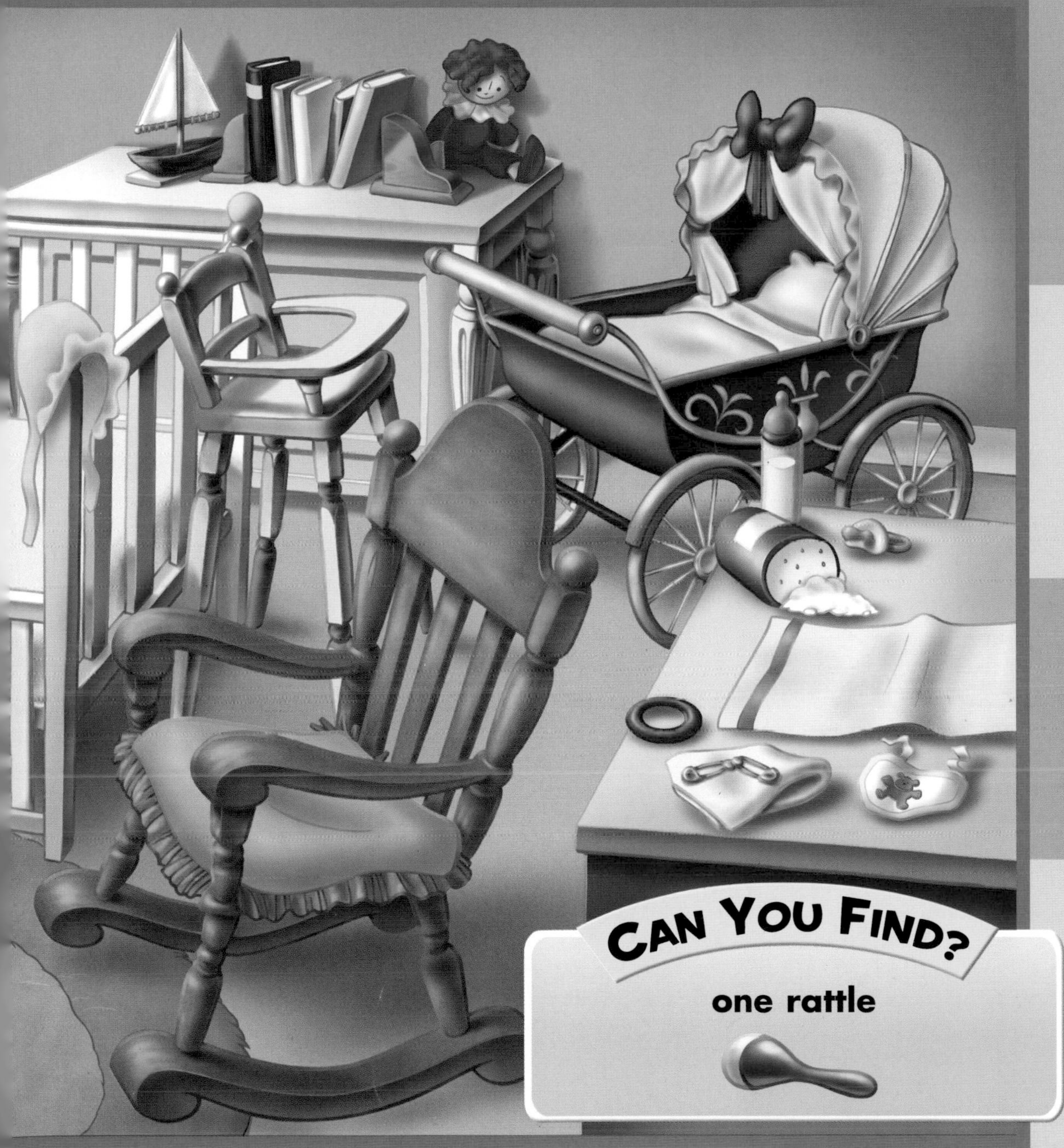

CAN YOU FIND?
one rattle

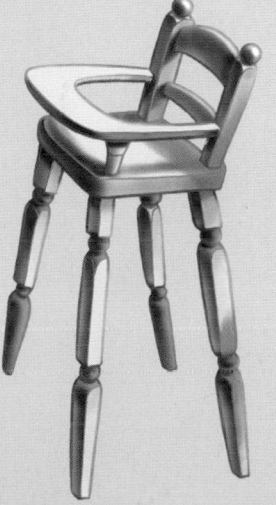
high chair

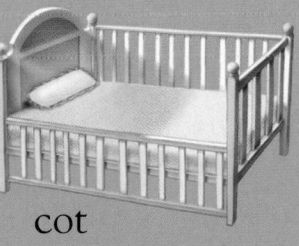
cot

talcum powder

teddy bear

31

Who's in Boo's Bedroom?

bedside table

pillow

picture

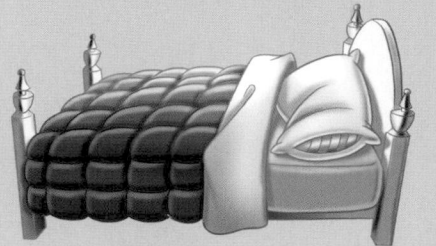

bed

telephone

carpet

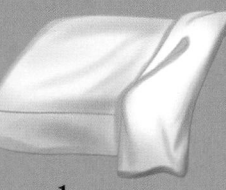

sheet

bedspread

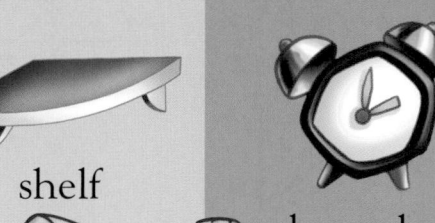
shelf

alarm clock

dressing gown

"Shh ! Sweet dreams, Boo!"

chest of drawers

toy box

blanket

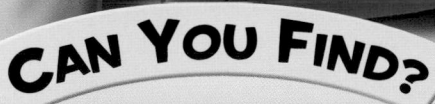
CAN YOU FIND?
two slippers
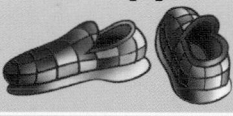

pillowcase

box

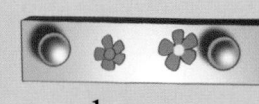
drawer

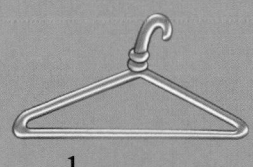
hanger

door

Cinderella Dresses the Mice

tiara

hat

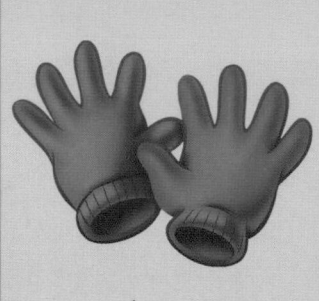

gloves

boots

suit

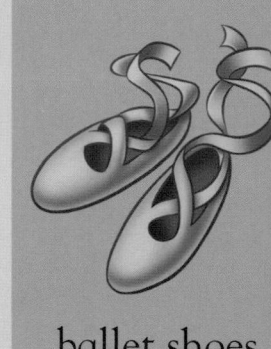

ballet shoes

coat

umbrella

jumper

skirt

high heels

gown

raincoat

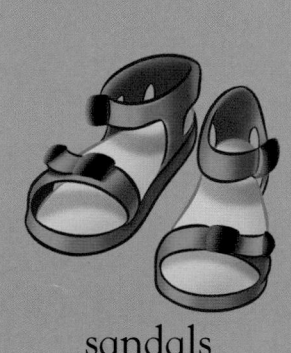

sandals

hair bow

cap

belt

scarf

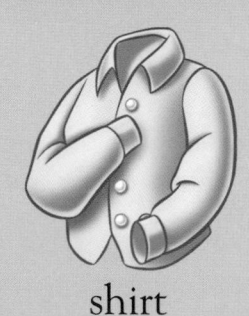

shirt

bow tie

socks

T-shirt

tutu

blouse

shoes

dungarees

tie

jacket

shorts

handbag

snowshoes

trainers

trousers

tuxedo

jeans

cloak

"Cinderellie, you have great taste in clothes!"

dress

mittens

"**W**elcome to our town!"

Town and

There's so much to do and see. What would

you like to do first? Would you like to see

or a ? Do you want to join and

as they post a letter at the post office?

Would you like to ride a or catch a

to visit Andy in his classroom? It

might be fun to talk to a or a

and learn what they do. Why not end

your adventure with and an ?

Community

Mickey and Friends Tour the Town

"There's so much to do in this town!"

bakery

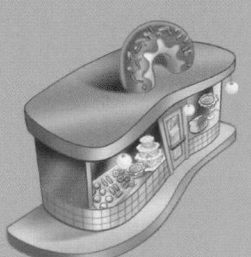

bank

bus stop

florist

dress shop

awning

magazine

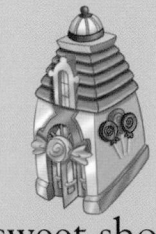

sweet shop

newsagent

lamp-post

road

department store

 cinema

 office building

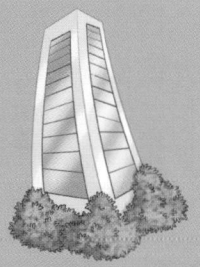 apartment building

 butcher

 restaurant

 newspaper

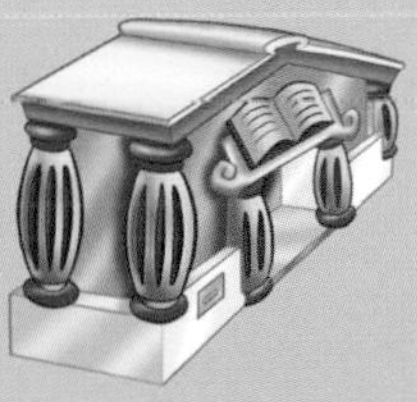

 library

grocery

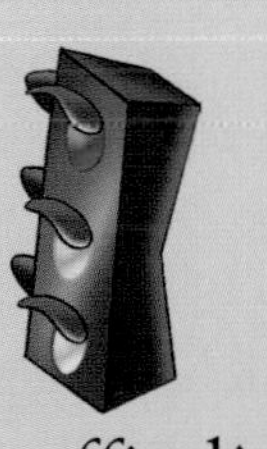

traffic light

Buzz Lightyear in the Toy Shop

CAN YOU FIND?

seven green soldiers

"We need to find Woody!"

electric train

dinosaur

action figure

piggy bank

soft toys

board game

jigsaw

chess

spinning top

bricks

doll

rocking horse

toys

spaceship

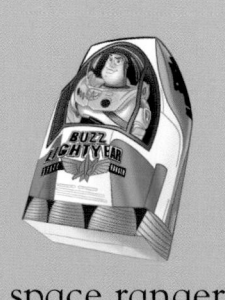

space ranger

dominoes

playing cards

telescope

draughts

41

Minnie at the Department Store

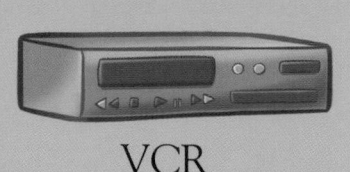
VCR

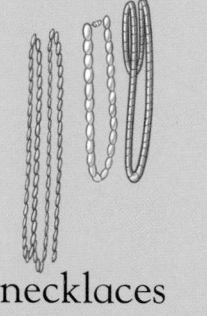
necklaces

screwdriver

drill

"What should I buy?"

pliers

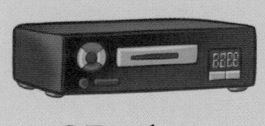
CD player

mouse mat

silver ring

mobile phone

bracelets

printer

radio

watch

calculator

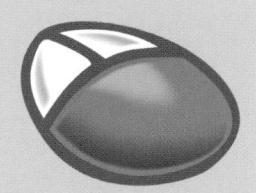
computer mouse

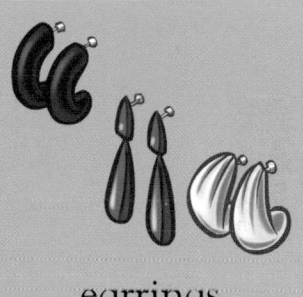
earrings

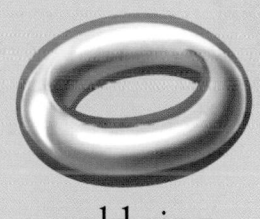
gold ring

video camera

CAN YOU FIND?

two nails

camera

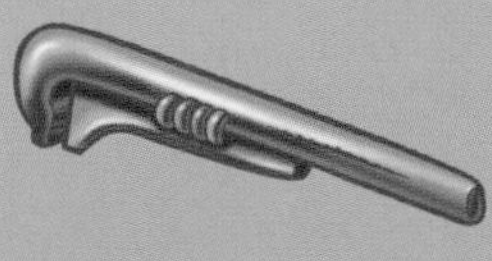

wrench

tape recorder

jewels

computer

43

Mike and Celia in the Restaurant

cashier

chopsticks
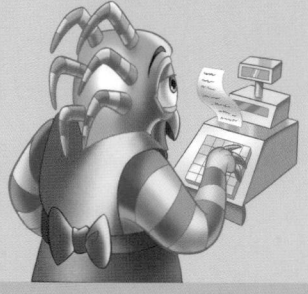

ice
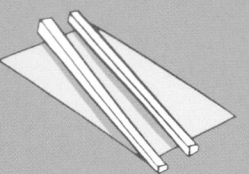

soy sauce

booth

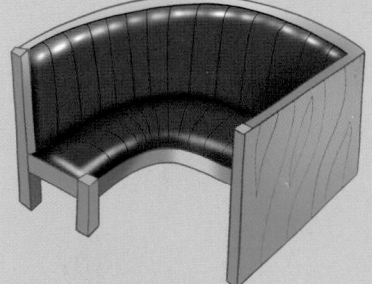

iced tea

money
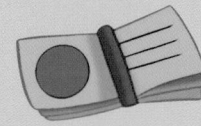

menu

jukebox

credit card

"Only the best for Schmoopsie... and you, too!"

MENU

waiter

counter

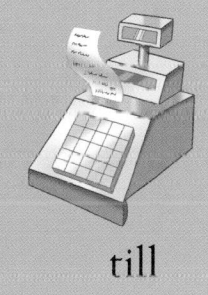
till

CAN YOU FIND?

four small fish

coins

wallet

sushi

bill

sushi chef

45

TOWN AND COMMUNITY

101 Dalmatians at the Sweetshop

"Mmm! I love ice-cream . . . don't you?"

CAN YOU FIND?

three cherries

maple syrup

muffins

doughnuts

biscuits

hundreds and thousands

croissants

cupcakes

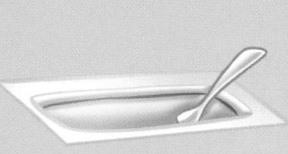
ice-cream

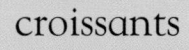
shortbread

ice-cream sundae

chopped nuts

hot chocolate

milkshake

whipped cream

sweets

crumpets

waffle

ice-cream cone

pie

fruit punch

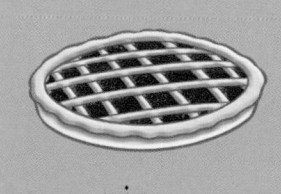

47

Lilo and Stitch at the Post Office

postage stamps

ink pad

notice board

clerk

address book

"It's fun at the post office!"

HAWAII

rubber stamp

envelope

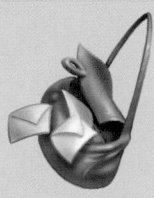

postbag

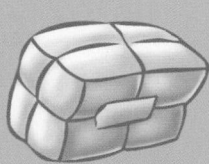

parcel

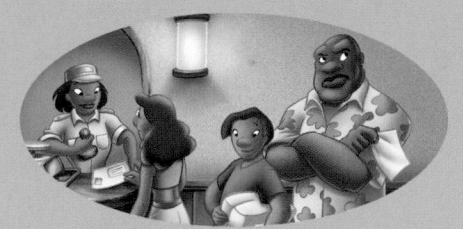

queue

address

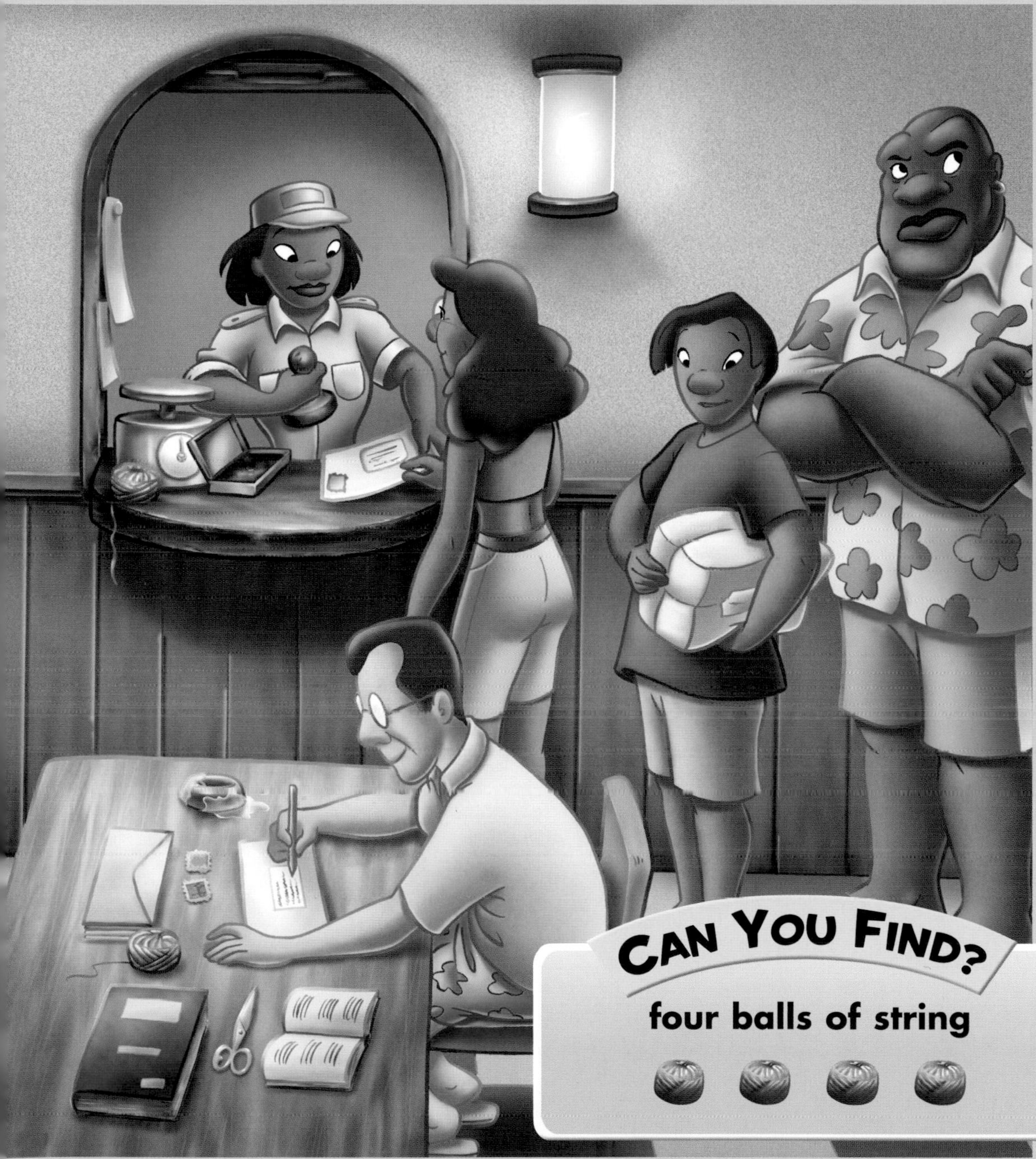

postman

letter

poster

CAN YOU FIND?

four balls of string

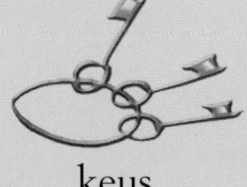

keys

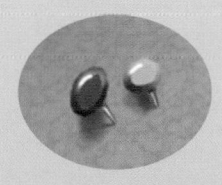

post

map pins

postcard

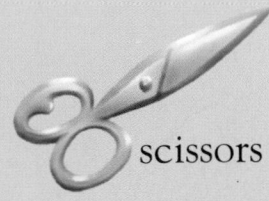

scissors

Buzz and Woody at Andy's School

"Look, there he is!"

teacher

graph paper

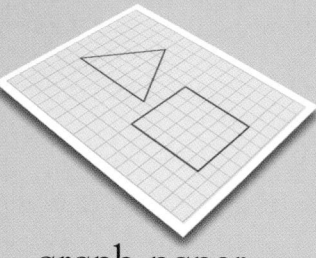

chalk

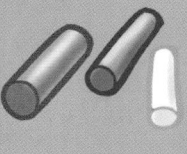

blackboard

comic

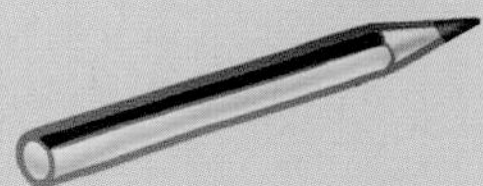

pencil

coat hooks

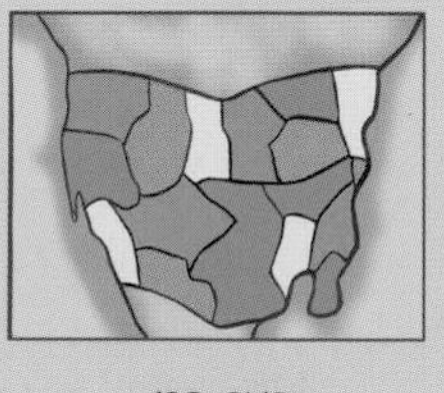

map

glasses

50

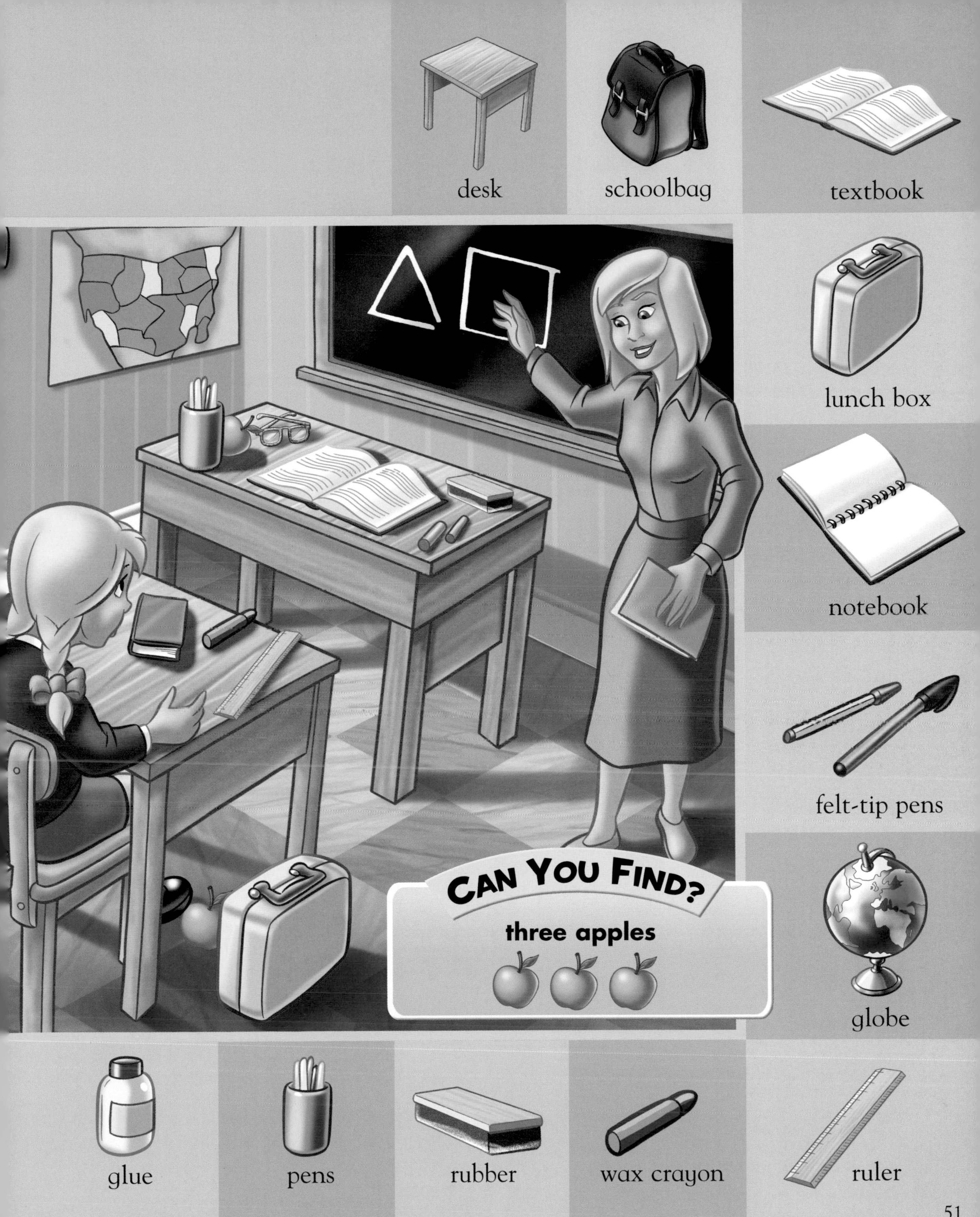

desk

schoolbag

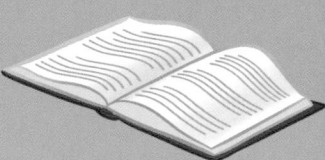

textbook

lunch box

notebook

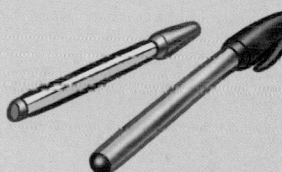

felt-tip pens

globe

CAN YOU FIND?

three apples

glue

pens

rubber

wax crayon

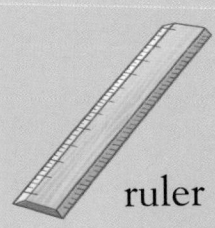

ruler

51

Lady and the Tramp at the Vet's

"We're here for a check-up!"

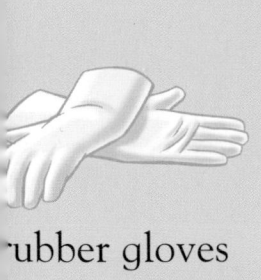 rubber gloves

 vet

 waiting room

 cotton-wool balls

 examining table

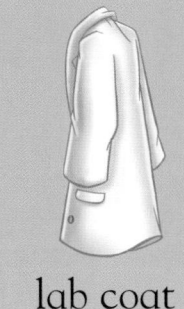 lab coat

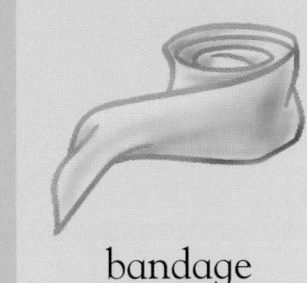 bandage

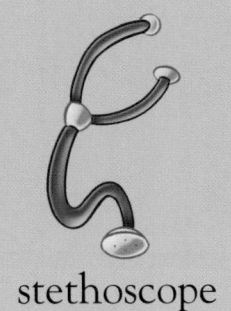 stethoscope

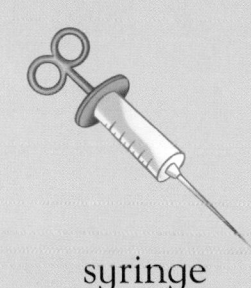 syringe

 dog collar

 mask

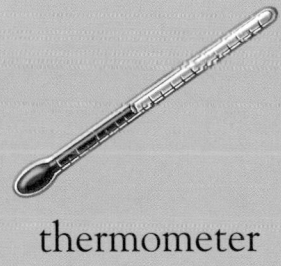 thermometer

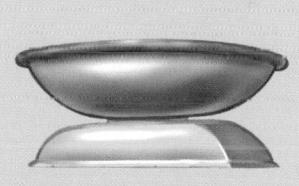 scales

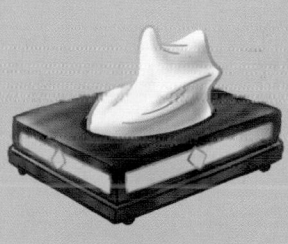 tissues

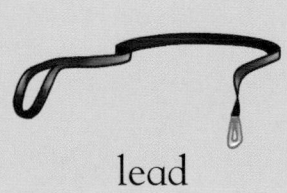 lead

 dog tag

 X-ray

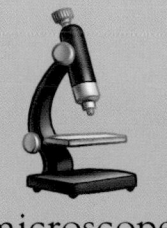 microscope

 filing cabinet

 file

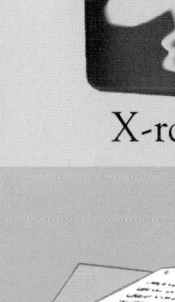

CAN YOU FIND?

four cotton-wool buds

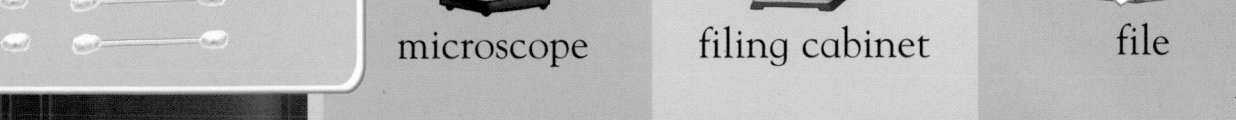

53

Donald Visits the Fire Station

fire station

chief fire officer

axe

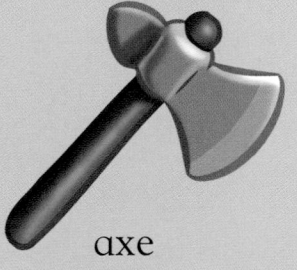

firefighter

water hose

wheel

fire engine

fire hydrant

steering wheel

ladder

bell

fire extinguisher

helmet

CAN YOU FIND?

three pairs of boots

pole

braces

loudspeaker

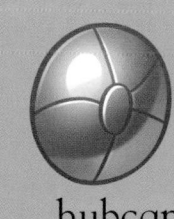
hubcap

alarm

Aladdin Takes a Ride

rowing boat

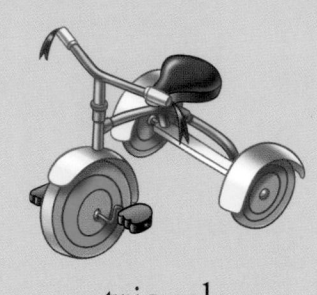

tricycle

tugboat

mobile home

double-decker bus

ferry

ambulance

houseboat

taxi

boat

bicycle

truck

removal van

submarine

tanker

motorcycle

hot-air balloon

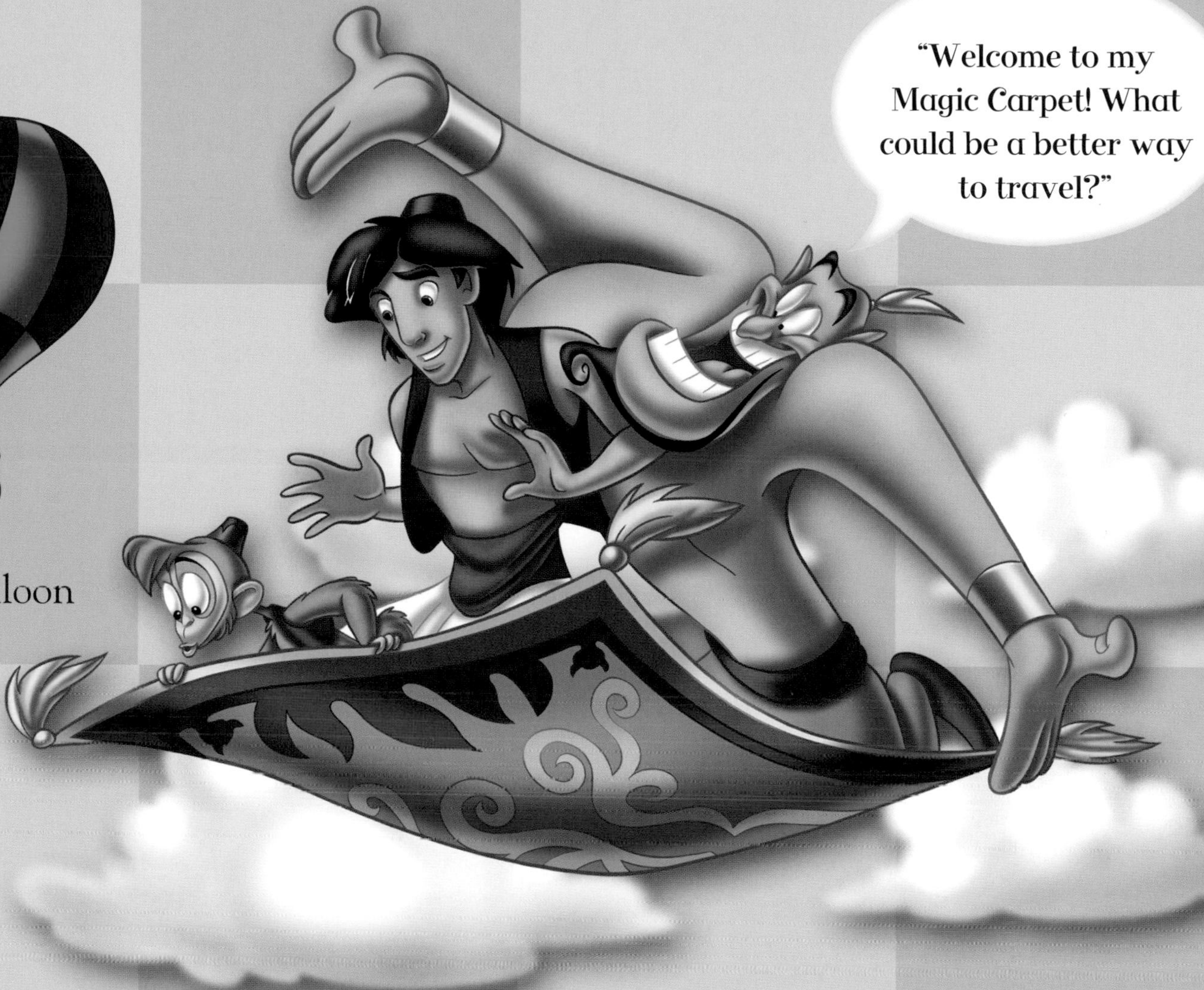

rocket

ice-cream van

cruise ship

police car

"Welcome to my Magic Carpet! What could be a better way to travel?"

school bus

train

tank

van

Buzz Finds a Toy Bulldozer

dumper truck

cement mixer

forklift truck

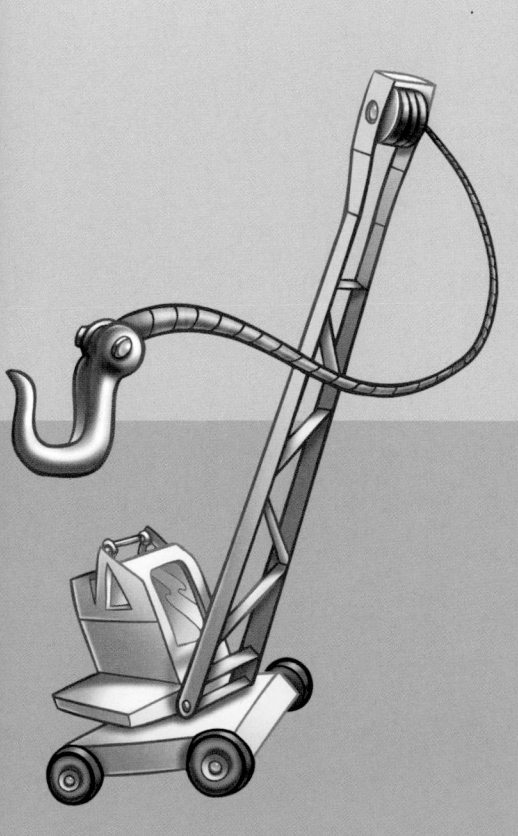

crane

bulldozer

tractor

snowplough

58

"Can you find another bulldozer? What else can you see?"

plough

road sweeper

tow truck

pick-up truck

garbage truck

steamroller

Mickey and Friends at the Airport

jet plane

customs

wing

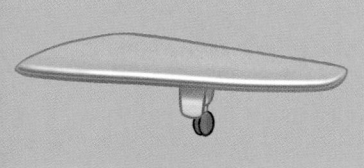

flight attendant

10

engine

propeller

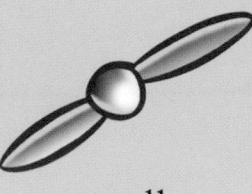

fuel tanker

pilot

suitcase

aeroplane

passport

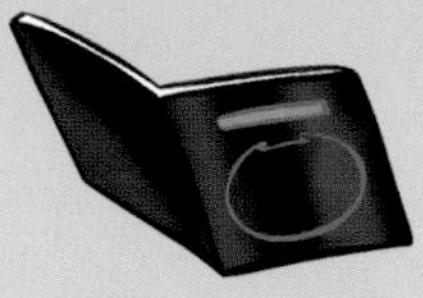

passenger

customs officer

control tower

"Wow! Look at all these passengers!"

ticket agent

check-in desk

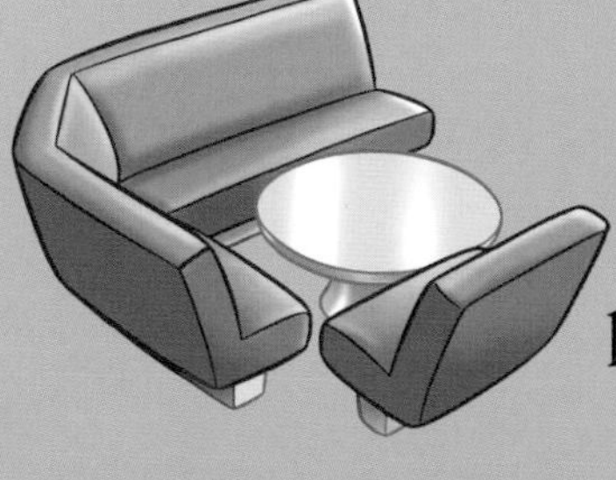

lounge

luggage label

tail

61

Monsters at Work

athlete

doctor

carpenter

police officer

TV presenter

ballet dancer

magician

sailor

librarian

photographer

chef

builder

bus driver

hairdresser

painter

cleaner

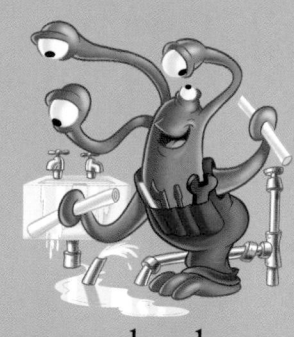

plumber

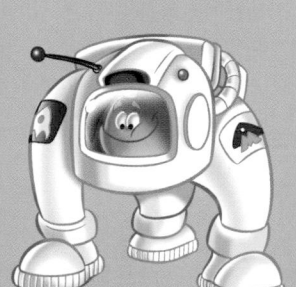

astronaut

secretary

nurse

doorman

dentist

car mechanic

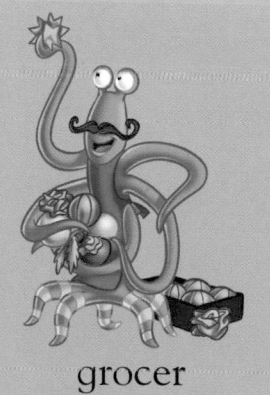

grocer

taxi driver

"What do *you* want to be when you grow up?"

Having Fun

"Hey, there! Are you ready to have some fun?"

Just turn the page and join   at the circus. Throw a ⚽ to 🦆. Dance with   . Pose for a picture with   . Go to the amusement park with   and taste some   . Then play on the beach, building a   with   . Have a great time!

Dumbo at the Circus

cage

big top

sword

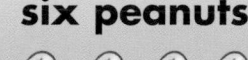

clown

top hat

ringmaster

megaphone

juggler

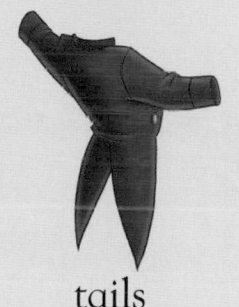
tails

feather

trapeze artist

tight rope

hoop

trapeze

lion tamer

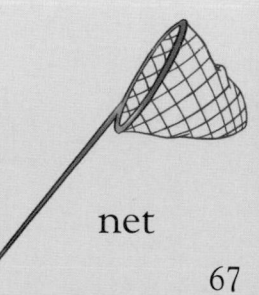
net

67

Pongo and Perdita at the Amusement Park

fun house

fudge

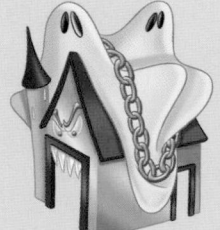

haunted house

dragon

"Wow, we can see everything from the big wheel!"

drawbridge

ticket

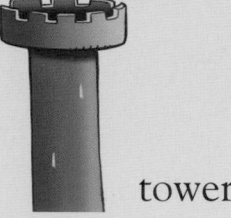

tower

ticket collector

monkey

fairy floss

organ grinder

big wheel

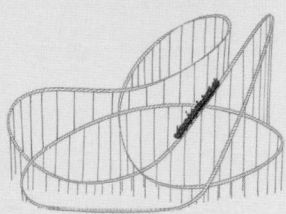
roller coaster

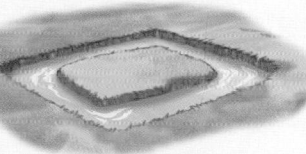
moat

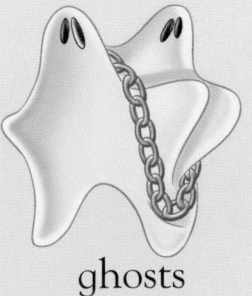
ghosts

CAN YOU FIND?

one cloth teddy bear

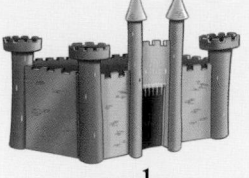
castle

carousel

crystal ball

fortune teller

pedalo

Playing in the Park with Lady and the Tramp

jogger

park

fountain

statue

kite

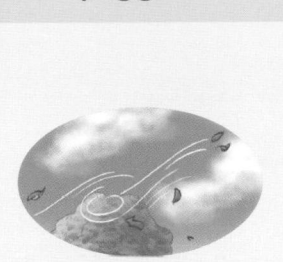

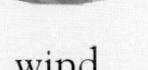

wind

birdbath

flag

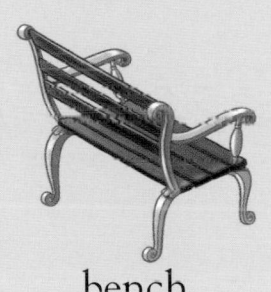

bench

pigeon

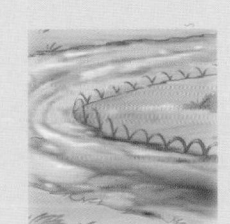

path

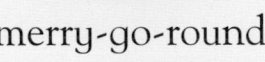

merry-go-round

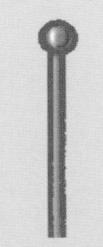

flagpole

rubbish bin

CAN YOU FIND?

Si and Am

string

71

HAVING FUN

At the Playground with Mickey

slide

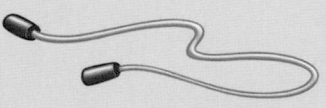

skipping rope

see-saw

swings

handle

rollerblades

hopscotch

72

spade

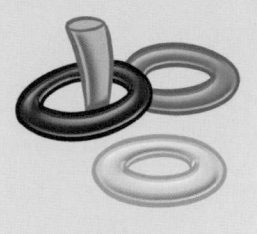

quoits

sandpit

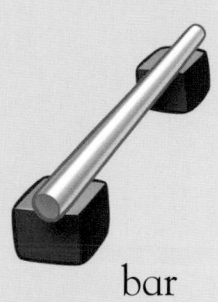

bar

tag

bucket

"Our uncle Mickey is the greatest!"

CAN YOU FIND?

two balls

skateboard

marbles

climbing frame

water fountain

Donald's Day of Sports

swimming

ice hockey

basketball

"Hey! Watch that ball!"

ice-skating

American football

74

tennis

hockey

polo

archery

table tennis

rowing

cycling

cricket

jogging

snowboarding

weightlifting

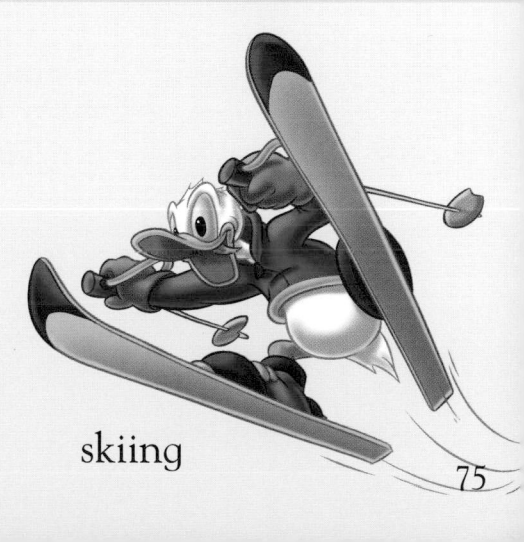

skiing

Miss Bianca Paints a Picture

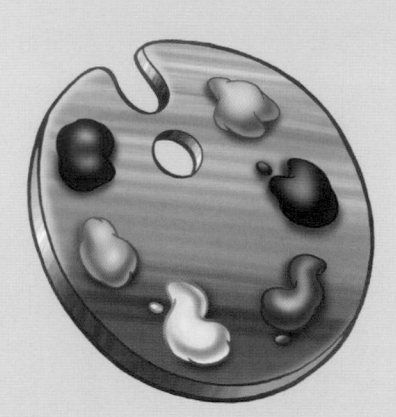

palette

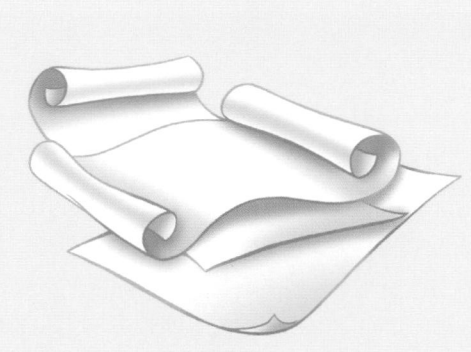

paper

artist

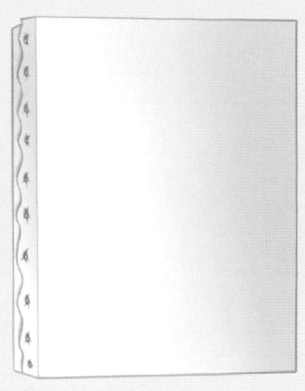

canvas

painting

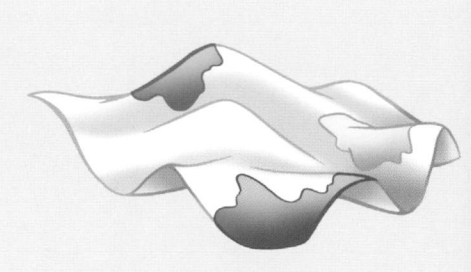

rag

sketches

paintbrush

portrait

clay

ceramics

pottery

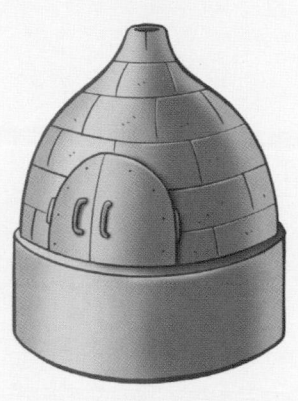

kiln

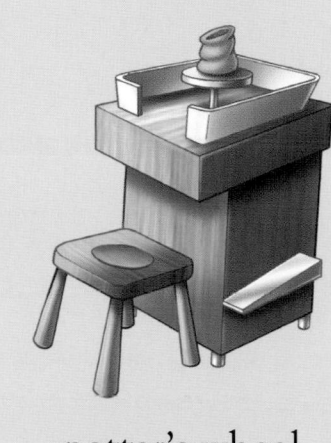

potter's wheel

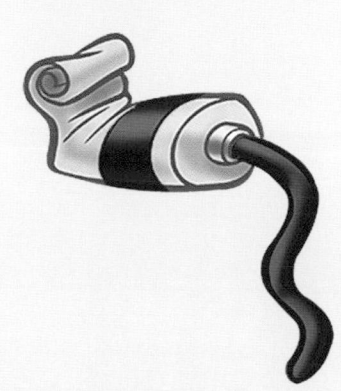

paint

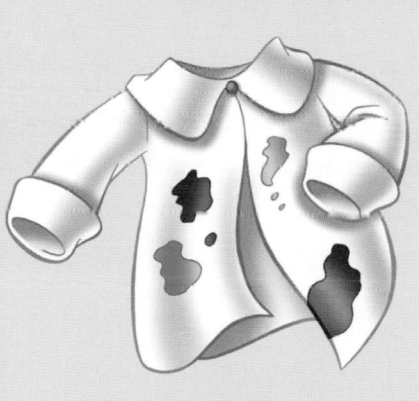

smock

easel

"I'd love to paint your portrait!"

The Aristocats
Move to the Music

piano

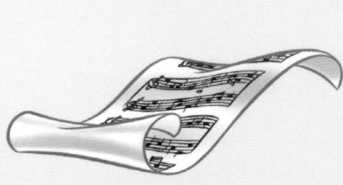

sheet music

trumpet

musical notes

piano keys

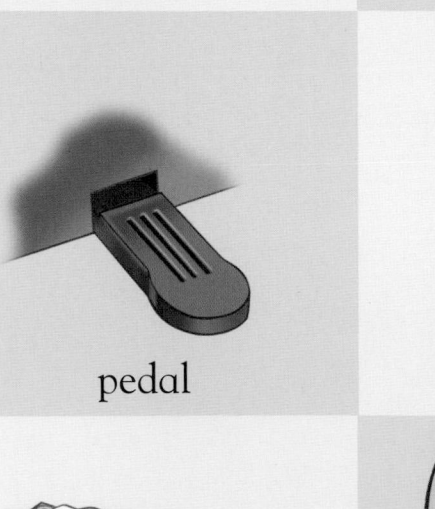

pedal

double bass

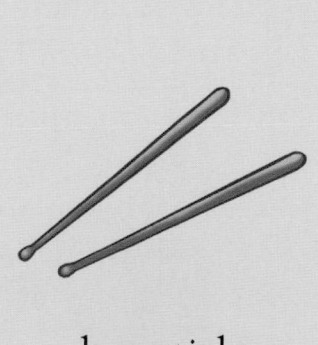

drumsticks

saxophone

flute

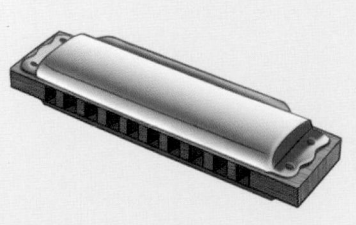

mouth organ

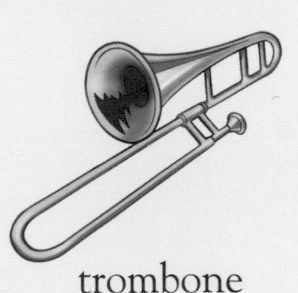

trombone

metronome

music
stand

guitar

drums

violin

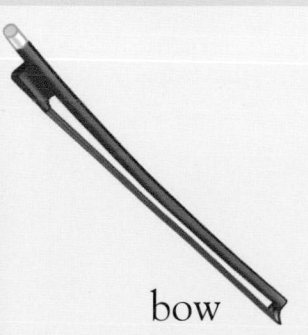

bow

musician

drummer

singer

79

baton

tuba

clarinet

piccolo

cymbals

tambourine

bugle

oboe

xylophone

bass drum

French horn

accordion

marching band

dancers

parade

confetti

81

Lilo and Stitch on the Beach

bathers

beach ball

surfboard

CAN YOU FIND?

two starfish

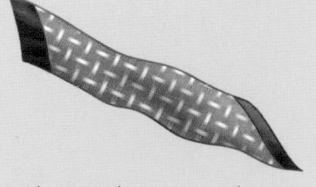

beach towel

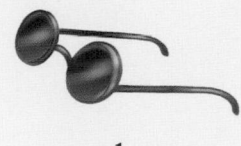

sunglasses

sun hat

beach

waves

swimming costume

sun cream

seaweed

lifeguard

"Surf's up! Come on in!"

sea

deckchair

umbrella

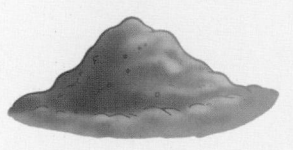

sand

seagull

shell

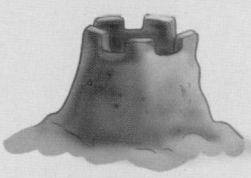

sandcastle

life jacket

Monsters, Inc.
at the Cinema

"I only have eye for Celia!"

screen

film

paper cup

row

popcorn

aisle

torch

film reel

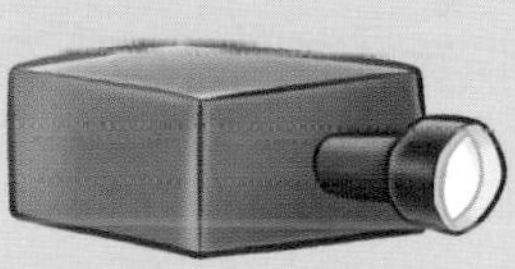

projector

usher

seat

CAN YOU FIND?
four cinema tickets

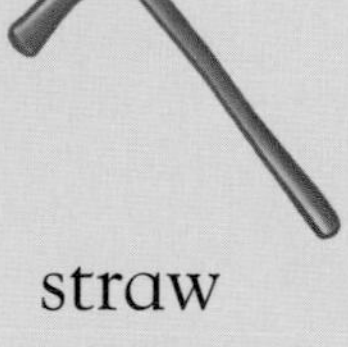

straw

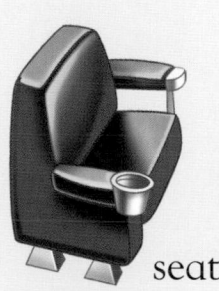
actors

drink

85

HAVING FUN

A *Toy Story* Birthday Party

BUZZ LIGHTYEAR SPACE RANGER

candles

paper plates

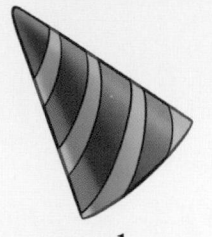
party hat

streamers

birthday cake

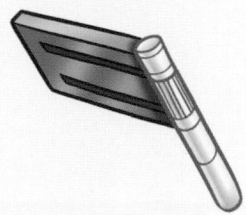
rattle

party whistle

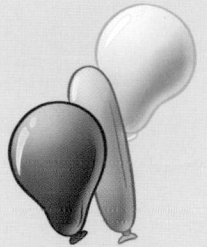
balloons

presents

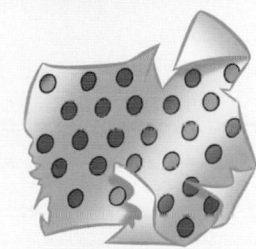
wrapping paper

ribbon

birthday card

CAN YOU FIND?

three pink ribbons

A Beauty and the Beast Christmas

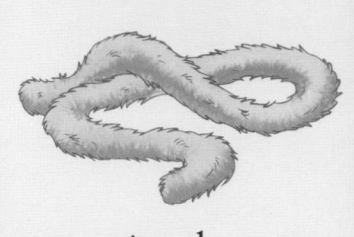

tinsel

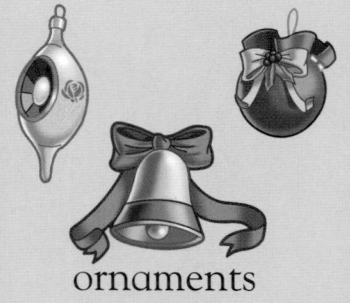

ornaments

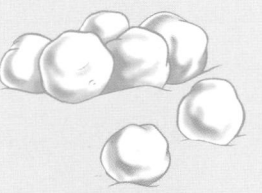

snowballs

wreath

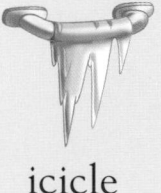

icicle

88

sledge

garland

angel

Christmas tree

muff

snowman

sleigh bells

"Don't you just love holidays!"

CAN YOU FIND?

eight pine cones

snowflake

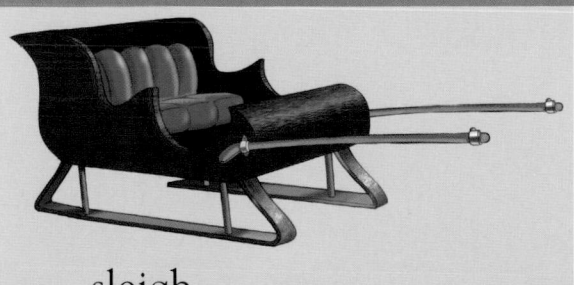

sleigh

popcorn chain

Animals

"Hello! Welcome to the great outdoors!"

and Nature

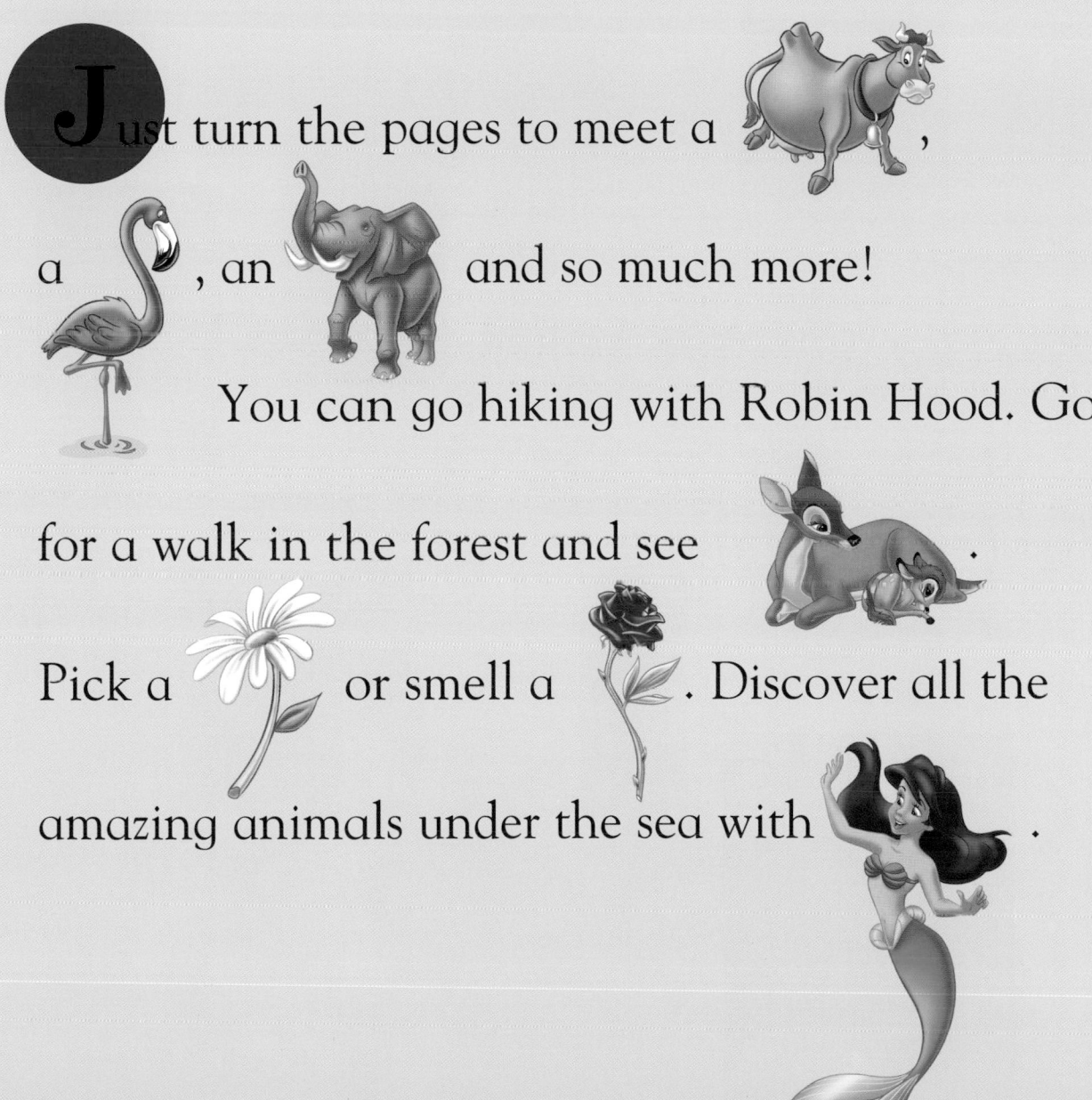

Just turn the pages to meet a cow, a flamingo, an elephant and so much more!

You can go hiking with Robin Hood. Go for a walk in the forest and see a fawn. Pick a daisy or smell a rose. Discover all the amazing animals under the sea with Ariel.

Lilo Goes to the Pet Shop

CAN YOU FIND?

three pet collars

"Will you help me choose the best pet?"

cat food

guinea pig

cat

puppies

turtle

rabbits

birdcage

goldfish

canary

fishbowl

aquarium

hamsters

dog

ferret

snake

iguana

kittens

101 Dalmatians
Visit the Farm

weather vane

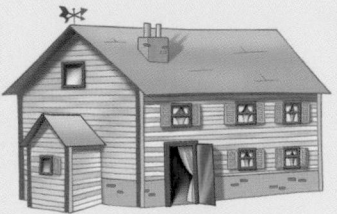

farmhouse

scarecrow

turkey

"Oh, no! The puppies have got out!"

duckling

goose

cow

goat

barn

piglet

chicks

cockerel

hens

lamb

CAN YOU FIND?

four eggs

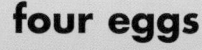

foal

kids

henhouse

donkey

hay

horse

calf

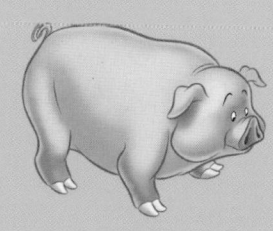

pig

sheep

ANIMALS AND NATURE

On the Plain with Simba

"Simba, everyone from the plain is here to greet you!"

gazelle

lion cub

gorilla

lion

CAN YOU FIND?

two of Zazu's loose blue feathers

rhino

chimpanzee

cheetah

hornbill

zebra

giraffe

baboon

wildebeest

elephant

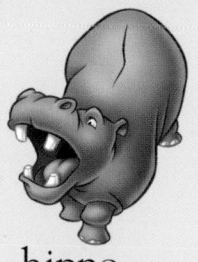
hippo

leopard

hyena

lioness

97

Lilo's Book of Wild Animals

crocodile

python

vulture

jaguar

poison-arrow frog

coyote

tarantula

grizzly bear

king cobra

tiger

Gila monster

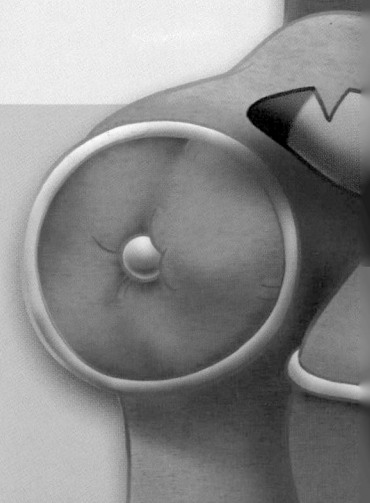

black panther

piranha

polar bear

black mamba

wolf

black widow spider

99

Zazu's Birds of a Feather

hawk

blue jay

penguin

flamingo

robin

bald eagle

toucan

hummingbird

magpie

swan

budgerigar

parrot

dove

bluebird

kingfisher

crow

pelican

puffin

stork

macaw

"Please! Help Simba find some other birds!"

ostrich

101

Bambi's Forest Friends

CAN YOU FIND?

five acorns

opossums

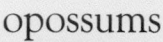

otter

moose

doe

butterfly

raccoon

fawn

porcupine

beaver

chipmunk

bird's nest

skunk

spider

spider's web

badger

owl

stag

fox

frog

squirrel

woodpecker

Goofy's Photo Safari

"L-l-look! I photographed these animals all by myself!"

giant panda

armadillo

orang-outang

hedgehog

manatee

walrus

chameleon

kangaroo

sloth

reindeer

anteater

camel

snail

koala bear

Ariel Plays in the Sea

seal

flounder

coral

clown fish

crab

shark

jellyfish

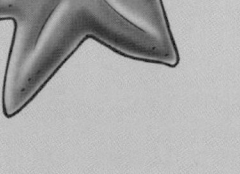

starfish

merman

octopus

dolphin

eel

whale

mermaid

squid

sea horse

minnow

sea turtle

Flik Finds the Circus Bugs

"I found the circus bugs! What can you find?"

bumblebee

grasshopper

cricket

rhinoceros beetle

ladybird

caterpillar

moth

stick insect

woodlouse

dragonfly

horsefly

ant

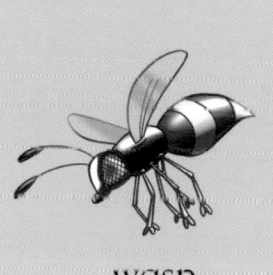
wasp

firefly

praying mantis

flea

daddy longlegs

greenfly

hornet

Robin Hood's Mountain Trail Adventure

stream

track

water bottle

rainbow

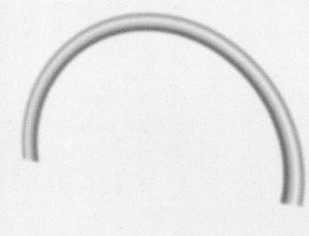

branch

cloud

roots

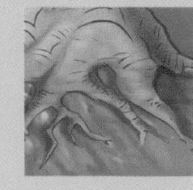

sky

tree

110

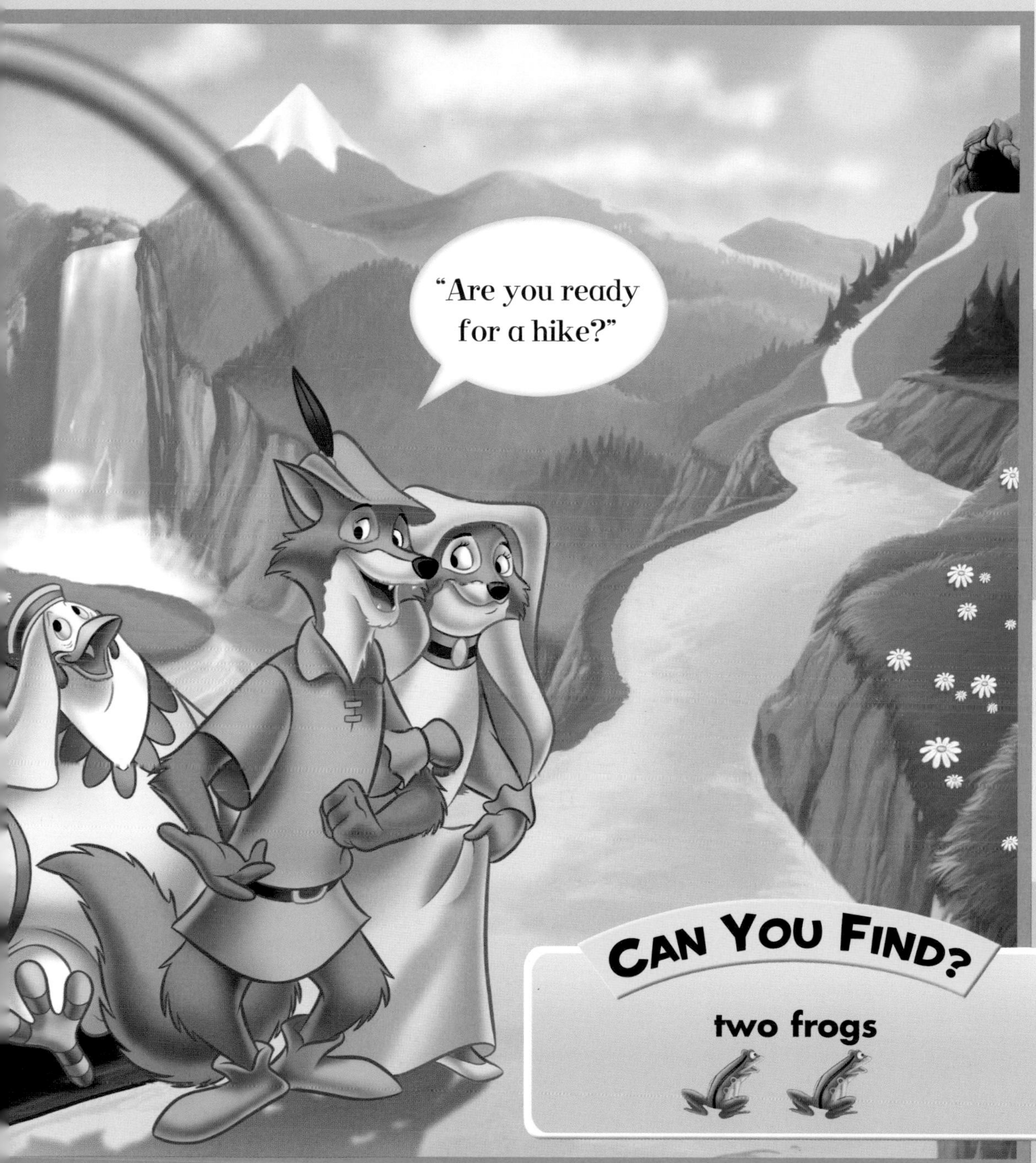

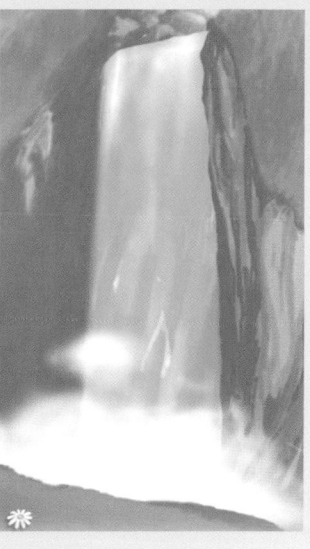

waterfall

mountain

cave

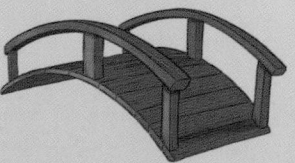

bridge

"Are you ready for a hike?"

CAN YOU FIND?

two frogs

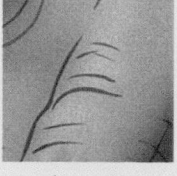

bark

sun

leaf

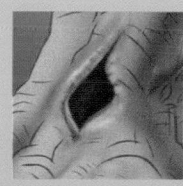

hole

shadow

Flower's Lovely Flowers

daisy

rose

lilac

tiger lily

dahlia

bluebell

carnation

tulip

baby's breath

orchid

poppies

violet

daffodil

wild flowers

pussy willow

"You can call me Flower if you want to!"

113

Peter Pan's Camping Trip

campfire

marshmallows

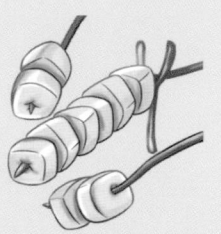

hot dogs

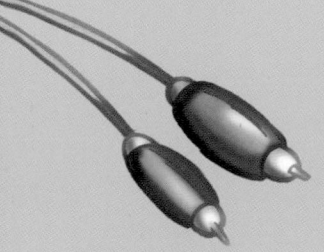

sleeping bag

"We're telling stories around the campfire. Would you like to hear one?"

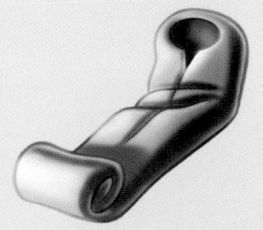

picnic basket

114

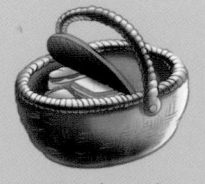

log

smoke

rocks

twigs

rope

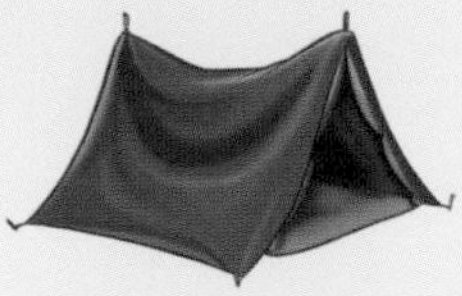

tent

beehive

grass

bushes

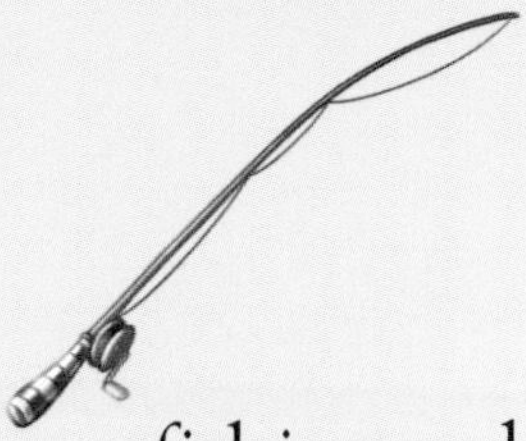

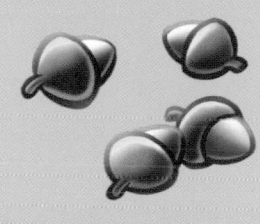

fishing rod

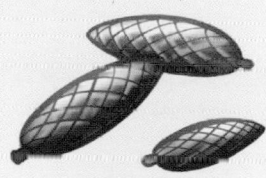

acorns

pine cones

anthill

CAN YOU FIND?

two pairs of yellow eyes hidden in the bushes

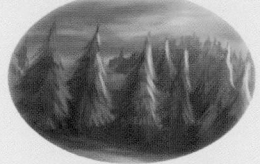

forest

moon

stars

bats

lantern

Things to

"It's nice to meet you! I'm a real boy now!"

Know

I can [dance]. In winter I get [cold] and just like you, I get [hungry]! Turn the pages to see colours like [orange leaf] and [red leaf]. Or use your [Pinocchio] to count numbers like [1] and [2]. Can you find shapes like a [heart] and a [circle]?

Whatever you do, just be happy!

Pinocchio Becomes a Real Boy

head

toes

ear

cheek

eyelashes

eyes

nose

chin

wrist

fingernails

neck

waist

thigh

leg

ankle

feet

118

hip

shoulder

hair

hands

arm

teeth

eyebrows

knee

tongue

fingers

elbow

mouth

119

THINGS TO KNOW

All Kinds of Feelings

sleepy

proud

silly

guilty

grumpy

sad

hungry

angry

scared

"Good morning, Snow White! You look cheerful today!"

Four Seasons with Bambi

spring rain

"The rain tastes so sweet!"

summer sunshine

"The flowers smell so good!"

autumn wind

"The wind sounds as if it's singing!"

winter snow and ice

"Whoa! This ice is slippery!"

THINGS TO KNOW

A Busy Year for Princesses

JANUARY	FEBRUARY
MAY	JUNE
SEPTEMBER	OCTOBER

124

MARCH	APRIL

JULY	AUGUST

NOVEMBER	DECEMBER

DAYS OF THE WEEK

Monday

Tuesday

Wednesday

Thursday

Friday

Saturday

Sunday

How Many Dalmatians?

1 one

2 two

3 three

4 four

5 five

6 six

7 seven

8 eight

9 nine

10 ten

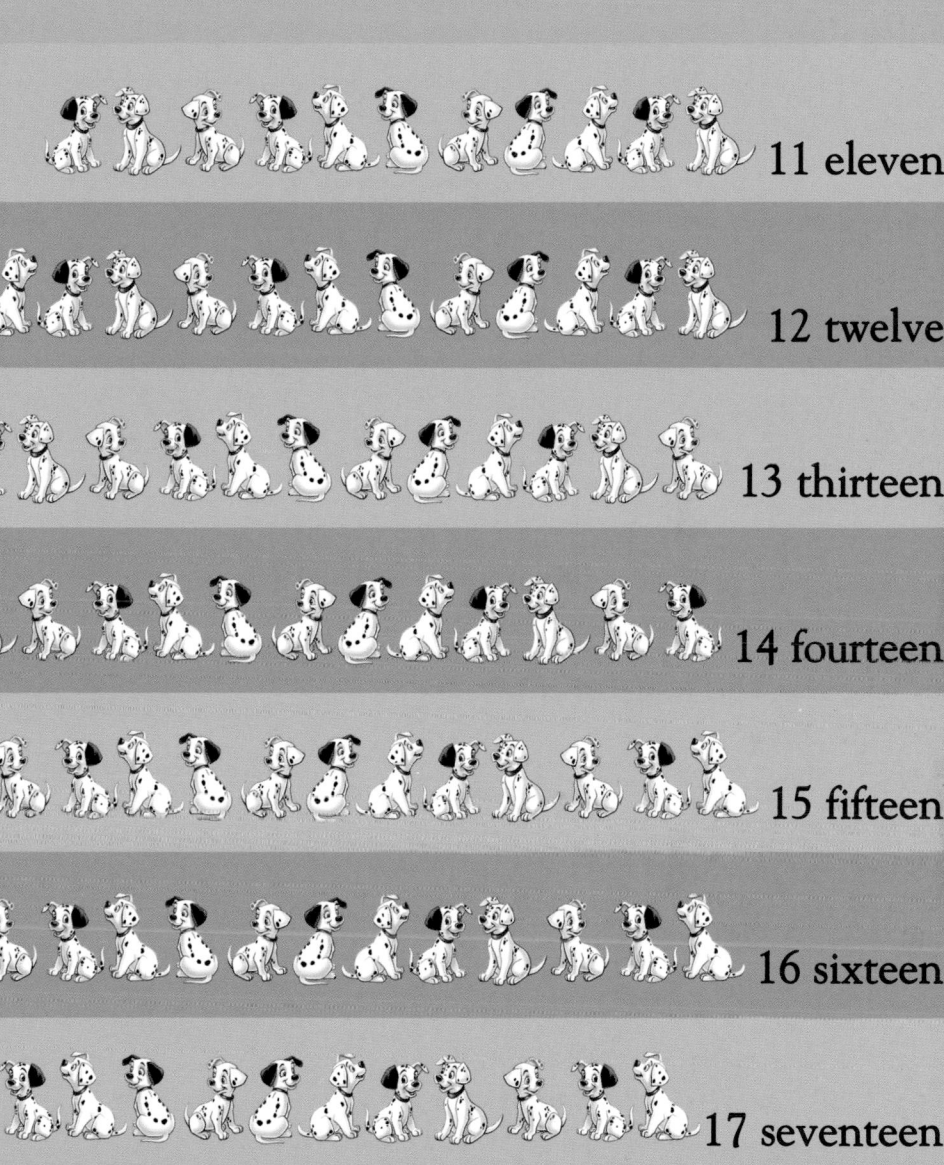

"How many puppies are there?"

11 eleven

12 twelve

13 thirteen

14 fourteen

15 fifteen

16 sixteen

17 seventeen

18 eighteen

19 nineteen

20 twenty

Finding Shapes in Wonderland

CAN YOU FIND?

four teacups

"How very curious things are here!"

rectangle

triangle

star

crescent

heart

diamond

oval

cone

cube

square

circle

THINGS TO KNOW

Pocahontas Sees Lots of Colours

white

red

pink

orange

yellow

purple

blue

grey

brown

CAN YOU FIND?

two sacks

green

black

131

THINGS TO KNOW

Aladdin's Favourite Opposites

big

small

"I'll catch you, you sneaky little monkey!"

bad

good

slow

fast

cold   hot

dry   wet

open   closed

fat   thin

quiet   noisy

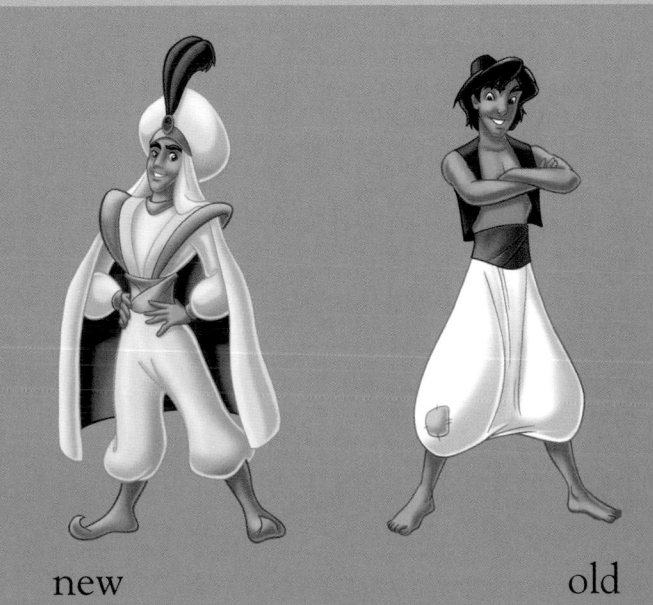

new   old

Busy Beauty, Busy Beast!

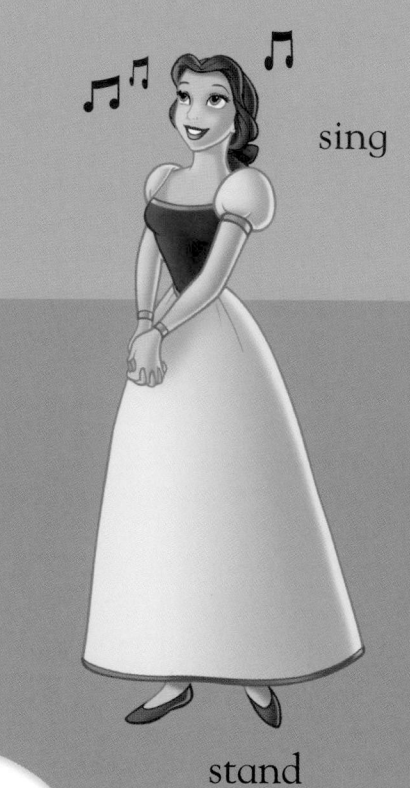

sing

clean

jump

stand

eat

"What things do *you* like to do?"

smile

talk

read

whisper

listen

think

write

laugh

sleep

sit

build

wake up

drink

kiss

run

dance

Hide-and-Seek with Simba and Nala

"I am left and Nala is right!"

left/right

far/near

below/above

through

in front of/behind

around

under/over

on/off

out/in

INDEX

139

Dalmatian	Goofy	Mike	Dumbo
Mrs Potts and Chip	Sulley	Pinocchio	Cinderella
Snow White	Tinker Bell	Mickey	Woody
Stitch	Timon	Mowgli	Aladdin